Where Is
New York?

Where Is
New York?

by Jennifer Marino Walters

illustrated by Ted Hammond

Penguin Workshop

To Keith Garton: For giving me my first
chance to write a children's book, I'll be
forever grateful!—JMW

PENGUIN WORKSHOP
An imprint of Penguin Random House LLC
1745 Broadway, New York, NY 10019
penguinrandomhouse.com

Designed and Produced by Dinardo Design, LLC.

Library of Congress Cataloging-in-Publication Data is available.

First published in the United States of America by Penguin Workshop, 2025

Manufactured in the United States of America
CJKW

ISBN 9798217051403 (paperback)
10 9 8 7 6 5 4 3 2 1

ISBN 9798217051410 (library binding)
10 9 8 7 6 5 4 3 2 1

The authorized representative in the EU for product safety and compliance is
Penguin Random House Ireland, Morrison Chambers, 32 Nassau Street,
Dublin D02 YH68, Ireland, https://eu-contact.penguin.ie.

Contents

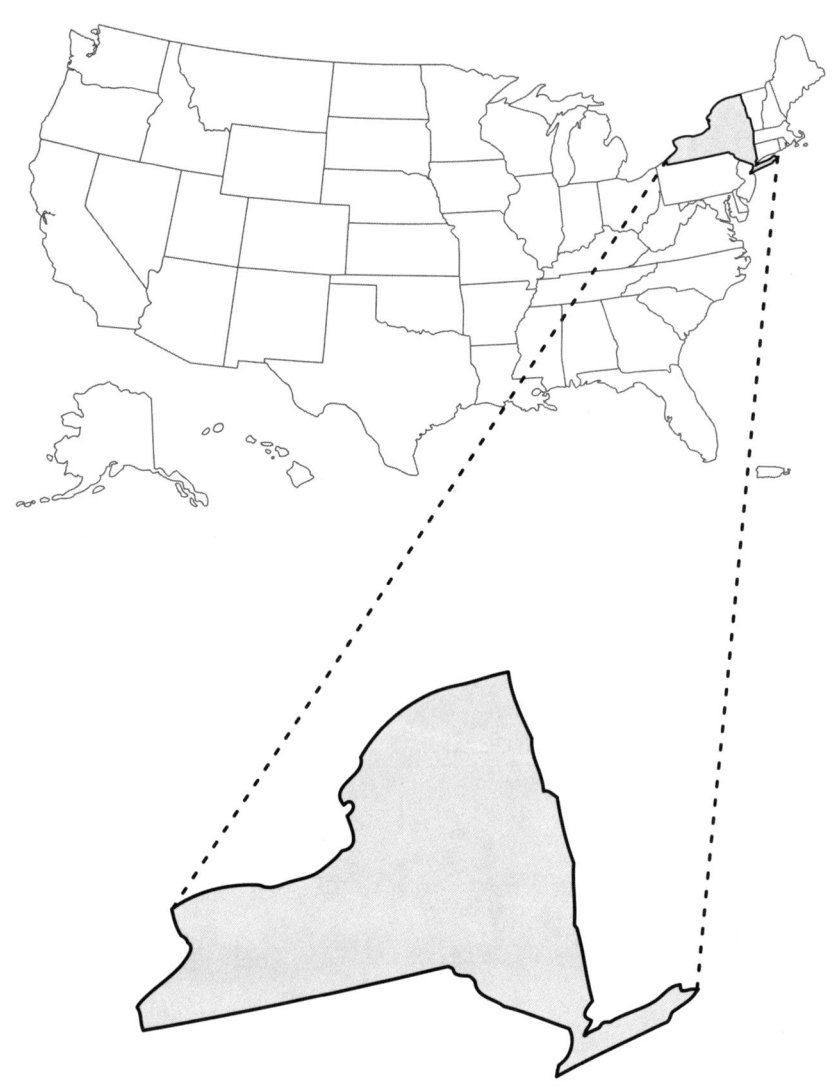

Where Is New York?

When people around the world think of the United States, they often picture New York. There's no doubt the state is famous all around the globe. In 2023 alone, more than 306 million people visited New York State.

New York wasn't the first US state—that honor belongs to Delaware. It is in the bottom half of the fifty states when it comes to size. And it's only the fourth most populous state in the nation (after California, Texas, and Florida). So, what is it that makes New York so special?

Whether it's Broadway musicals, New York Fashion Week, or the *New York Times* newspaper, New York has always been an international center for culture. For hundreds of years, immigrants from all over the world settled in New York. From the skyscrapers of Manhattan to the snow-capped Adirondack Mountains to the towering Niagara Falls, it's a place where different landscapes, people, and cultures come together to make something completely unique—New York.

CHAPTER 1
New York's Land and Beginnings

New York was one of thirteen British colonies established on the Atlantic coast of North America. A year after the start of the Revolutionary War, the United States adopted the Declaration of Independence from England on July 4, 1776. After winning the war in 1781, the United States went on to write its Constitution in 1787. Delaware was the first colony to officially ratify, or approve of, the Constitution and become a state. The other colonies followed over the next two-and-a-half years. New York was the eleventh colony to declare statehood. It became a US state on July 26, 1788.

New York is located in the Northeastern United States. Today, it is bordered by Pennsylvania and

New Jersey to the south; Vermont, Massachusetts, and Connecticut to the east; and Lake Erie, Lake Ontario, and the country of Canada to the west and north. While it has a long history, New York State doesn't set any records for size or population. At 54,555 square miles, it's the twenty-seventh largest US state. With just under twenty million people living there as of 2023, New York is the fourth most populous state.

New York City is record-setting, though. It has been the most populous city in the United States since the first US census (a count of the country's population) was held in 1790. It's also the most densely populated US city, with about 43 percent of all New Yorkers living in the city's 305 square miles. Many of these people live close together in apartment buildings or townhouses. New York City is over ten times more populous than the

state's second-most populous city, Hempstead. Yet it makes up less than one percent of the total land area of New York State!

Located at the southern tip of the state, New York City is part of the Hudson-Mohawk Lowland. Within this area lies the Hudson Valley and the Mohawk Valley. Part of the New York City area, Long Island and Staten Island are in a flat region called the Atlantic Coastal Plain. Long Island is at the most southeastern part of the state and is bordered by the Atlantic Ocean and the Long Island Sound. Long Island has many white-sand beaches with big waves.

The areas north and west of New York City are known as upstate New York, or simply "upstate." In fact, most of New York is upstate, including its capital city, Albany. New York has four distinct seasons: hot and humid summers, cold winters, and mild springs and autumns. The areas around Syracuse, Rochester, and Buffalo in upstate New York receive heavy amounts of snow.

New York's largest region is the Appalachian Highlands, which makes up about half the state. This area extends west from the Hudson Valley to the southern and western parts of New York. The Catskill Mountains (which reach up to four thousand feet) and the Finger Lakes (a group of eleven narrow lakes) are part of this area.

North of the Appalachian Highlands and west of the Mohawk Valley is a flat region called the Erie-Ontario Lowlands. These Lowlands are home to plains that border the Great Lakes. A large variety of fruits are grown there, including grapes, peaches, apples, and cherries.

Bodies of water of all kinds crisscross New York. The state is home to more than 7,500 lakes, ponds, and reservoirs, as well as over seventy thousand miles of rivers and streams. There are over two thousand waterfalls across New York State. The most dramatic—and most famous—is

Niagara Falls, located in the northwestern part of the state, along its border with Canada. Made up of three waterfalls—Horseshoe Falls, American Falls, and Bridal Veil Falls—Niagara Falls is one of the most popular tourist attractions in the country. Niagara Falls State Park, established in 1885, is the oldest state park in the United States.

More than 60 percent of New York State is covered in forests. These forests contain nearly 150 species of trees. The most common variety are Norway maples. Cairo, New York, about two hours north of New York City by car, is home to the oldest known forest in the world. The forest has been around for about 385 million years and survives in a fossilized, or preserved, form, usually as impressions in rocks. Scientists have learned about ancient plants from this "forest," including how early trees grew seeds.

Indigenous groups have been living in the area now known as New York for at least thirteen thousand years. The Mohican (say: mo-HEE-kin) and Munsee Nations spoke a language called Algonquian (say: al-GON-kwee-in) and lived near the Atlantic coast. The five nations of the Iroquois (say: IR-uh-kwoy)—the Mohawk, Oneida (say: oh-NIGH-duh), Onondaga (say: ah-nuhn-DAH-guh), Cayuga (say: kay-YOO-guh), and Seneca Nations—made their homes in the central and western parts of the state.

Italian explorer Giovanni da Verrazzano was the first European to reach New York. Sailing for France, he entered New York Bay on April 17, 1524 and landed on the tip of what is now Manhattan, in New York City. He then continued northward to explore more of America's eastern coast. In 1609, English explorer Henry Hudson sailed into New York Bay. He was working for a Dutch shipping company to try to find faster routes from Europe to Asia. Hudson explored the river that is now named after him.

He realized it could provide a route to inland fur-trading posts.

Furs of North American mammals were very valuable, especially beavers, whose pelts (or skins) were waterproof and used to make hats. When Henry Hudson arrived in North America, beavers had been hunted nearly to extinction in Europe. This inspired Dutch merchants to travel to New York to explore fur trading with the Mohawk, the Mohican, and other Indigenous peoples.

The Dutch set up the first permanent European settlement in New York in 1624. The settlement was called Fort Orange and was located in the east central part of the state along the Hudson River. Today, the city of Albany stands there. In 1625, the Dutch established New Amsterdam—now New York City—on the southern end of Manhattan Island. Several other Dutch trading posts sprouted up along the Hudson River.

The English also wanted to be part of the fur trade. A fleet sent by James II, Duke of York, sailed into New York Harbor in 1664 with the aim of taking over New Amsterdam. This settlement would enable them to control the entrance to the Hudson River, an important North American trade route. Peter Stuyvesant (say: STY-vuh-sint), the Dutch governor of New Amsterdam, couldn't urge enough citizens to fight for the land, so he surrendered to the English. With the area now in England's control, New Amsterdam was renamed New York in honor of the Duke of York.

The British continued their control into the

1770s, but the New York colonists were angry because they wanted to be self-governing. Along with twelve other British colonies, they rebelled, and the American Revolutionary War began in 1775. Nearly one-third of all Revolutionary War battles took place in New York. Though the war did not end until 1783, the United States declared independence from England in 1776.

Many Indigenous people and groups clashed with the New York colonists, who were eager to expand their settlements in Indigenous lands. Colonists brought deadly diseases to Indigenous nations and often didn't honor their agreements. All of the Iroquois Nations except the Oneida fought on the side of the British during the Revolutionary War. When the war was over, settlers forced Iroquois people out of New York. Many of them resettled in Canada.

CHAPTER 2
New York City: A Land of Opportunity

In 1788, New York City was established as the first capital of the United States. George Washington was sworn in there as the first US president in 1789. After temporarily moving the capital from New York City to Philadelphia, the federal government moved the capital to Washington, DC, in 1800.

Albany became New York's state capital in 1797. It was chosen because of its location on the Hudson River and because it has been a trading and military center during the Revolutionary War.

By the mid-1800s, America's—and New York's—population exploded with the arrival of new immigrants. From 1845 to 1852, Ireland experienced a mass starvation event known as the Great Famine or the Irish Potato Famine. Blight (plant disease) was ruining potato crops in Ireland. At the time, all of Ireland was controlled by Great Britain.

Even though potato crops had been Ireland's main food source before blight had struck, the British government continued to export much of Ireland's remaining food. As a result, Irish people starved. Nearly two million Irish people came to America from 1845 to 1852 to escape the crisis.

Italy was also experiencing famine at this time, along with earthquakes and other natural disasters. In Russia, Jewish people suffered persecution for their religion and were beaten or killed. Other European immigrants came to the United States from countries like England, Greece, Hungary, Germany, and Poland to escape joblessness and poverty and to seek religious freedom.

America was a land of promise. Factories were opening in big cities like New York City. Land out west was selling for low prices. People longed for a steady job, enough food to eat, freedom to practice their religion, and a home to call their own. At the time, the United States had an "open door policy." That meant there were no controls on immigration. Anyone who wanted to come was welcome. Individual states, not the national government, were responsible for keeping track of immigrants.

Some Americans became concerned about immigration. The government passed laws that were racist and xenophobic (prejudiced toward people from other countries), such as the Chinese Exclusion Act, which barred Chinese immigrants from entering the United States.

In 1890, the US government took over control of immigration. Laws were passed to exclude immigrants who were sick or who had been convicted of crimes. Despite these discriminatory laws and the new rules limiting the number of immigrants, people still came. Between 1880 and 1920, more than twenty million immigrants arrived in the United States.

The government needed a place for these new people to enter the country. It chose a tiny island off New York City called Ellis Island. On January 1, 1892, Ellis Island opened as an immigration station to welcome these newcomers, largely from Europe. The immigrants crammed onto crowded steamships and traveled across the Atlantic Ocean for seven to ten days to get to America. The journey was long and extremely difficult. But to many, it was worth it. America meant freedom, safety, and jobs. It meant a new life for them and their families.

One of those immigrants was a teenaged Irish girl named Annie Moore. She traveled alone with her two younger brothers, aged eleven and seven, to meet their parents in the United States. Annie was the first immigrant to set foot on Ellis

Island the day it opened. She and her brothers settled with their parents in New York City, in a neighborhood called the Lower East Side. About one-third of the immigrants who arrived at Ellis Island stayed in New York City. Millions of them settled on the Lower East Side, like Annie's family.

There, life wasn't easy. Immigrant families lived in small, three-room apartments in crowded

buildings called tenements. Some blocks had over four thousand residents, with up to ten people sleeping in one room. Thousands worked in small New York City factories called sweatshops. They made very little money. Even children had to work. Nearly two million kids aged five to fourteen had full-time jobs in factories, mines, and other places!

Lady Liberty

The millions of immigrants arriving at Ellis Island were welcomed by a towering symbol of American freedom—the Statue of Liberty. Dedicated on October 28, 1886, the massive copper statue offered a message of hope to the new immigrants. It also welcomed American soldiers returning home after World War I and World War II.

The Statue of Liberty was designed and sculpted by French sculptor Frédéric-Auguste Bartholdi (say: fred-eh-REEK aw-GOOST-uh bar-TOHL-dee). It was given to America as a gift from the people of France to honor the friendship between the two countries. Its distinctive green color comes from the copper it's made from oxidizing (being exposed to the oxygen in the air).

Located on Liberty Island in New York Harbor, the Statue of Liberty stands 151 feet, one inch tall (roughly the height of thirty-five eleven-year-old kids stacked head to toe). Add in its foundation and pedestal, and the total height is about 305 feet!

Today, the Statue of Liberty is one of the most visited landmarks in the United States. About four million people take special ferries to it each year. Some of them even climb the 354 stairs to the statue's crown! They also visit the Statue of Liberty Museum, which opened on Liberty Island in 2019.

People leaned on each other to get through their hard days. They spent a lot of time outside, speaking to each other in their native languages. They sold and cooked foods from their home countries. Some US citizens didn't like that. They were prejudiced against them. They wanted the immigrants to speak English, give up their ways of doing things, and fully adopt American culture. They wanted the United States to be a "melting pot," where cultures blended together into one.

Over time, most of the immigrants' lives improved. In many of their home countries in Europe, only rich people could afford school, but public school was free in America. Immigrant children learned English, received an education, and grew up to get better jobs and make easier lives for themselves than their parents had.

Ellis Island remained open as an immigration station until November 12, 1954. By that time, about twelve million immigrants had passed through it to make a new life in America. Forty percent of today's Americans—over one hundred million people—can trace their history to Ellis Island! Ellis Island is now a national monument. The main building is a museum. Over two million people visit Ellis Island every year, and a statue of Annie Moore stands there today.

CHAPTER 3
An Expanding New York

While New York City grew, people also settled in other parts of the state. In the early 1800s, settlers began to move westward across New York State thanks to the construction of large roads called turnpikes. Later, railroad systems were also created.

The opening of the Erie Canal in 1825—a waterway from the Atlantic Ocean to the Great Lakes—connected New York City to cities in the western part of the state like Rochester, Buffalo, and Syracuse. This added to population spread. By the turn of the century, more and more wealthy and middle-income white people began to move out of New York City and into the surrounding suburbs. Many also moved upstate as more transportation routes were built.

Other Americans were also moving to New York. From about 1916 through 1970, over six million Black Americans moved from the South to cities in the North, Midwest, and West. This is known as the Great Migration. These Americans were fleeing racism, lack of economic opportunity, and southern laws that required segregation (the separation of Black and white people in public places like schools and buses). They also wanted to take advantage of the factory jobs that had emerged during World War I in northern cities.

Many of these Black Americans settled in a northern Manhattan neighborhood, Harlem. Between 1910 and 1920 alone, New York City's Black population grew 66 percent. This led to a cultural and artistic explosion in the 1920s and 1930s known as the Harlem Renaissance.

During the Harlem Renaissance, Black writers like Langston Hughes and Zora Neale Hurston

Duke Ellington performing

wrote proudly about the African American experience. Jazz music soared in popularity, with famous musicians like Louis Armstrong and Duke Ellington performing in Harlem. African American theater and art became increasingly popular.

Buffalo is another city where many European immigrants and Black Americans made their homes. It is on the border of New York and Canada, very near Niagara Falls. The Erie Canal made it an important inland port for shipping grain and milling (or grinding) flour. After the introduction of the railroad, the city became a hub for train shipment and travel, as well as manufacturing cars and airplanes. Many people went to Buffalo seeking work. World War II, which took place from 1939–1945, created a demand for ships, airplanes, and weapons, which Buffalo's factories produced.

Not everyone came to New York to live there—

some people came to visit! Twice, New York State hosted the Olympic Winter Games in Lake Placid, first in 1932 and again in 1980. Located in northeastern New York, Lake Placid is among the Adirondack Mountains, the highest mountain region in New York. For over one hundred years, the Adirondacks have been a popular place to hike, ski, and spend time among high peaks (like

Mount Marcy, New York's highest) as well as beautiful freshwater lakes.

Known for its cold, snowy winter weather, it's no wonder that Lake Placid hosted the Winter Games twice. The 1980 Lake Placid Olympic games are perhaps most remembered for the "Miracle on Ice." This nickname refers to the US men's hockey team's win over the USSR. (The

USSR, or Union of Soviet Socialist Republics, was sometimes called the Soviet Union. This country existed from 1922 to 1991 and included what are now many countries in Europe and Asia, like Estonia, Russia, and Kazakhstan.) The USSR team had been dominant in men's hockey for decades and Olympic champions since 1964. The US team went on to win gold despite being huge underdogs!

After the Olympics, the state also invested in an Olympic training center for athletes from the United States who want to compete in future Olympic games. Structures like the alpine ski jump still stand in Lake Placid. Tourists visit the region not only for its beautiful scenery but also for its history.

CHAPTER 4
Today's State

Sports and international events are big reasons that New York State grew to have one of the largest economies in the world. Many important sporting events are held in New York, including the US Open Tennis Championships in Queens and the Belmont Stakes horse race. Cooperstown in central New York is home to the National Baseball Hall of Fame.

New York also depends on farming for its economic success. Today, nearly one-third of the state's land area is farmland, including cropland and dairy farms. Many fruits and vegetables are grown there, including apples, cherries, tomatoes, peas, sweet corn, strawberries, and more. New York is the second largest producer of maple syrup

(after Vermont) and cabbage (after California) in the United States.

Manufacturing is still happening in upstate New York. Photographic equipment, heavy machinery, instruments, and paper products are some of the items most frequently produced there. And New York's capital, Albany, is at the center of an area known as Tech Valley, where many technology companies are located.

The heart of New York's booming economy is New York City, which is considered the world's biggest financial center. It's home to the New York Stock Exchange, as well as banks and financial institutions and companies. Many of them are located in the Financial District of Lower Manhattan.

September 11, 2001

On September 11, 2001, members of a terrorist group called al-Qaeda hijacked four airplanes. They flew two of these airplanes into the Twin Towers, part of the original World Trade Center in Lower Manhattan. These 110-story skyscrapers were once the tallest buildings in the world.

Soon after the hijacked planes hit the towers, they collapsed. Over 2,700 people died, including 147 on board the planes. (A third hijacked plane hit the Pentagon in Washington, DC, killing all 64 people on board and 125 people in the Pentagon, a building that serves as the headquarters for the US Department of Defense. A fourth plane crashed into a field in Pennsylvania after its forty passengers and crew members fought back against the hijackers. Everyone on board was killed.) This horrible event changed New York, and the world, forever.

One World Trade Center

New Yorkers came together and vowed to bounce back even stronger. They helped with search and rescue efforts, donated blood, provided medical help, and more. And bounce back, New York did. The new One World Trade Center, also known as the Freedom Tower, was completed in 2014. At 1,776 feet tall, it's the tallest skyscraper in the Western Hemisphere.

New York City has been called the media capital of the world. Many of the biggest book and magazine publishers and TV studios are based there. Some of the best-known newspapers, including the *New York Times* and the *Wall Street Journal*, are created there.

New York City has a huge fashion industry and a thriving arts scene. There are over 170 museums in the city, including the Metropolitan Museum of Art and the American Museum of Natural History. The city is known for its theater, centered around Broadway—the area between Forty-Second and Fifty-Third Streets. Many famous singers and bands have gotten their start at the city's various music clubs. And some of the greatest musicians in the world have played the famous concert venue Carnegie Hall, from classical composers like Pyotr Tchaikovsky (PYOH-ter chy-KOF-skee) to legendary bands like the Beatles.

All of these things have earned New York City a nickname as the City That Never Sleeps. That's especially true during the holiday season, when visitors flock to New York City to see the iconic Rockefeller Center Christmas tree, the Radio

City Christmas Spectacular at Radio City Music Hall (featuring the world-famous Rockettes), and the decorated store windows along Fifth Avenue, a shopping destination.

With so much to see and do in New York City, the tourism industry is huge. Over sixty million people visit New York City each year to see famous places like the Empire State Building, Central Park, Times Square, and the United Nations headquarters. While there, they can snack on the city's famous pizza and bagels.

Since many of today's New Yorkers were born in other countries or have parents who were born outside the United States, visitors can choose from a huge variety of food. They can try authentic Chinese food in Lower Manhattan's Chinatown, eat delicious pasta on Arthur Avenue in the Bronx, sample soul food in Harlem, and much, much more.

Some of the most common countries of origin

for New York City residents are the Dominican Republic, China, Jamaica, Mexico, Guyana, and Ecuador. About eight hundred languages are spoken in New York City alone!

New York has the second-highest Puerto Rican population of any state (after Florida) and more Dominican Americans than any other state. The Bronx, Manhattan, Brooklyn, and Queens have large Dominican American populations. New York has the country's second-highest population of Asian Americans (after California) and one of the highest populations of African Americans. Cuban, Colombian, Mexican, Ecuadoran, and other Hispanic groups also moved to New York City in large numbers in the 1990s. Today, it is estimated that almost one-fourth of New York City residents speak Spanish at home.

Because of New York City's diverse population, all sorts of multicultural festivals and celebrations take place there. These include the National

Puerto Rican Day Parade each June in Midtown Manhattan, the Feast of San Gennaro every September in Lower Manhattan's Little Italy, and Midtown's St. Patrick's Day Parade in March.

Many students of various backgrounds also come to New York to attend college. The state has over two hundred colleges and universities. Several of New York's universities are ranked among the top schools in the country and the world. These include Cornell University in Ithaca and Columbia University in New York City. And the State University of New York (SUNY) is one of the largest public university systems in the United States. It includes sixty-four colleges and universities. The United States Military Academy (USMA) at West Point is in the Hudson Valley, about fifty miles north of New York City. Founded in 1802, it's one of the oldest service academies in the world. USMA prepares students to become US Army officers.

New York City itself has the largest metro transportation system in the country, which includes the New York City subway, buses, and railroads. They connect the five boroughs that make up New York City—Manhattan, Brooklyn, Staten Island, Queens, and The Bronx. Bridges connect the tiny island of Manhattan to the other

boroughs. These include one of the most famous bridges, the Brooklyn Bridge, opened in 1883. The New York City area is also home to three of the busiest airports in the country!

It's no wonder that so many famous people have called New York home, including former presidents like Theodore Roosevelt, Franklin

Delano Roosevelt, and John F. Kennedy. With so many professional sports teams in New York, many well-known athletes live in the state at least part of the time. Teams include Major League Baseball's New York Yankees and New York Mets; the National Basketball Association's New York Knicks and Brooklyn Nets; the National Hockey League's New York Rangers, New York Islanders, and Buffalo Sabres; the National Football League's New York Giants, New York Jets, and Buffalo Bills; the Women's National Basketball Association's New York Liberty; and Major League Soccer's New York Red Bulls and New York City FC.

Even New York City's skyline, with hundreds of towering skyscrapers, is famous. The city has been immortalized in countless movies, TV shows, books, and songs, from Frank Sinatra's "New York, New York" to Alicia Keys's "Empire State of Mind."

No matter where in the state they live,

New Yorkers can trade the hustle and bustle of Manhattan for the quaint beaches of the Hamptons on Long Island. They can swap the calm waters of the Finger Lakes for the raging rush of Niagara Falls. And they can leave the rolling hills of the Hudson Valley and head to the towering peaks of the Adirondacks or Catskills. New York State truly has it all!

New York at a Glance

Statehood: 1788

Nickname: The Empire State

Abbreviation: NY

State Motto:
Excelsior (Latin for
"ever upward")

State Tree: Sugar
Maple

State Animal: Beaver

Capital: Albany

Size: 54,555 square miles

Population: Over 19 million

Famous People from New York:

Billy Joel (singer), Kareem Abdul-

Jabbar (former NBA player),

Lady Gaga (singer and actress),

Maurice Sendak (author)

★ Albany

State flag

State flower
Rose

State bird
Eastern bluebird

FUN FACT:

At six million acres, Adirondack Park in eastern upstate New York is the largest state park in the United States. It's one of 180 state parks in New York.

Timeline of New York

1524	Italian explorer Giovanni da Verrazzano lands on the tip of Manhattan
1609	Sailing for the Dutch, Henry Hudson explores the river that's later named for him
1625	New Amsterdam colony is established on Manhattan Island
1664	The British take control of New Amsterdam and rename it New York
1788	New York becomes the eleventh US state
1797	Albany becomes the capital of New York
1825	The Erie Canal opens, connecting New York City to Buffalo and the Great Lakes
1883	The Brooklyn Bridge is opened
1886	The Statue of Liberty is dedicated on October 28
1892	Ellis Island opens and goes on to welcome over twelve million immigrants
1932	Lake Placid hosts the Winter Olympics for the first time
1954	Ellis Island closes as an immigration station
1980	Lake Placid hosts the Winter Olympics for the second time
2001	The Twin Towers collapse in the terrorist attacks of September 11
2024	The New York Liberty win the WNBA championship

Timeline of the World

1503–1519	Leonardo da Vinci paints the *Mona Lisa*
1620	The *Mayflower* arrives in Plymouth Harbor in Massachusetts
1648	India's Taj Mahal is completed
1787	The US Constitution is signed, establishing the government of the United States
1861	The US Civil War begins
1893	New Zealand becomes the first country to give women the right to vote
1912	The *Titanic* sinks on its maiden voyage from England to New York City; more than 1,500 people drown
1929	The Great Depression begins in the United States after the New York Stock Exchange crashes
1965	The Immigration Act of 1965 ends quota laws on US immigration
2008	Barack Obama is elected the first African American US president
2010	The Burj Khalifa is completed in Dubai, becoming the tallest building in the world
2024	The ruins of a roughly 2,500-year-old city are discovered in eastern Ecuador

Bibliography

*Books for young readers

*Brennan Demuth, Patricia. *What Was Ellis Island?* New York: Penguin Workshop, 2014, 2023.

*Crane, Cody. *My United States: New York (A True Book)*. New York, NY: Scholastic Inc., 2017.

*Holub, Joan. *What Is the Statue of Liberty?* New York: Penguin Workshop, 2014.

*Mattern, Joanne. *Ellis Island: Gateway to America*. South Egremont, MA: Red Chair Press, 2018.

*Mattern, Joanne. *The State of Liberty: A Welcome Gift*. South Egremont, MA: Red Chair Press, 2018.

*O'Connor, Jim. *What Were the Twin Towers?* New York: Penguin Workshop, 2016.

Websites

Official website of the 9/11 Memorial & Museum: www.911memorial.org

Official website of Ellis Island: www.statueofliberty.org

Official website of the Empire State Building: www.esbnyc.com

Official website of the Statue of Liberty: www.nps.gov/stli/index.htm